Karen's OMG Joke Book for Kids

Funny, Silly, Dumb Jokes that Will Make Children Roll on the Floor Laughing

Karen J. Bun

Table of Contents

Bluesource And Friends

This book is brought to you by Bluesource And Friends, a happy book publishing company.

Our motto is **"Happiness Within Pages."**

We promise to deliver amazing value to readers with our books.

We also appreciate honest book reviews from our readers.

Connect with us on our Facebook page www.facebook.com/bluesourceandfriends and stay tuned to our latest book promotions and free giveaways.

Don't forget to claim your FREE book

https://tinyurl.com/karenbrainteasers

Also check out our best seller book

https://tinyurl.com/lateralthinkingpuzzles

Introduction

Congratulations on downloading the book *Karen's OMG Joke Book for Kids: Funny, Silly, Dumb Jokes that Will Make Children Roll on the Floor Laughing*. I thank you for downloading it. The following chapters will make your child howl with laughter. The first chapter is filled with riddles that will make their sides hurt. This book has everything from the classic knock-knock jokes to bad puns that will make even you shake your head! There are also a few surprises along the way! Your child will read some 'quirky questions' as well as 'books never written.' This book was designed for kids between the ages of seven and twelve. They will experience short, sweet, and simple jokes as well as longer jokes that grab their attention and deliver a forceful one-liner!

There are plenty of books like this on the market, so thanks again for choosing this one! Every effort was made to ensure your child will enjoy what they are about to read. Please enjoy!

Chapter 1 Kids' Riddles

Q: My outside can be thrown and my inside can be cooked. My outside can be eaten and my inside can be thrown. What am I?

A: A corn's cob. The stalk is thrown and the corn is cooked. The inside can be thrown once the corn has been eaten.

Q: I have three hands but I cannot use them to clap. What am I?
A: I'm a clock.

Q: You can only use me once you have broken me. What am I?
A: I'm an egg.

Q: I can't see even though I still have an eye. What do you think I am?
A: A needle

Q: The most water can only be held by what letter?
A: The 'C'

Q: There was a blue, one-story house. The couch was blue. The rugs were blue. Even the cat was blue. What color do you think the stairs were?

A: The house didn't have any stairs. It was only one-story.

Q: All through winter, I have lived. Once I die during summer, roots start to grow from the top. What am I?
A: An ice cycle

Q: Even the world's strongest person can't hold this for more than sixty seconds although it is as light as a feather. What is it?
A: They can't hold their breath.

Q: A cowboy rode into town on Wednesday. He stayed for three days and left the same town on Wednesday. How can this be possible?
A: The cowboy's horse's name is Wednesday.

Q: How is it possible for a person to go without sleep for 8 days straight?
A: They only sleep at night.

Q: Moneyless people have this and it is needed by wealthy people. You will eventually die once you've eaten it. What is it?
A: It's nothing.

Q: Which has more weight, a pound of cement or a pound of paper?
A: Both of them weigh a pound, so they are equal.

Q: What is used more by other people but is always yours?

A: Your name

Q: I can't open doors even though I'm full of keys. What am I?

A: I'm a piano.

Q: I have four fingers and one thumb, but I am not a living thing. What am I?

A: A glove

Q: How many months in the year have twenty-eight days in them?

A: All of the months have twenty-eight days!

Q: Which invention helps you to see through walls?

A: A window

Q: What occurs one time in a minute, two times in a moment, and never in 100 years?

A: 'M'

Q: As it dries, it gets wetter?

A: A towel gets wetter as it dries.

Q: Everyone has one of these, and it is impossible to lose. What is it?

A: A shadow

Q: How much distance can be run by a fox into the woods?
A: Only halfway. Otherwise, it would be running out of the woods.

Q: Take away a single letter, I become even. At first, I'm very odd. What am I?
A: Seven

Q: This will never fall back down but will always go up.
A: Your age

Q: What word has a T and starts and ends with a T?
A: It's a teapot.

Q: I get shorter as I get old, although when I was young, I am tall. What am I?
A: A candle

Q: What word is spelled wrong in every single dictionary?
A: Wrong

Q: I start with the letter 'E', and I only have one letter in me. What am I?
A: I'm an envelope.

Q: How does a leopard change its spots?

A: It gets up and moves to a different one.

Q: What is really hard to get out of but super easy to get into?

A: Trouble

Q: If a mom, a dad, and their son were not underneath an umbrella, how did they not get wet?

A: It wasn't raining.

Q: Troy's parents had three sons. They were named Snap, Crackle, and what?

A: Troy

Q: You bought me for dinner, but you have never eaten me. What am I?

A: A fork and knife

Q: After a train crashed, every single person died. Who survived?

A: All of the couples

Q: I still can't see even though I have four eyes.

A: Mississippi

Q: Even though I'm staying in the same spot, I can still travel all around the world. What do you think am I?

A: A stamp

Q: The English alphabet contains how many letters?

A: There are eighteen. 3 in 'the', 7 in 'English', and 8 in 'alphabet'.

Q: I can still hold liquid even though I have holes. What am I?

A: A sponge

Q: What can you never answer yes to?

A: Are you asleep?

Q: When everything seems to be going wrong, what can you always count on?

A: Your fingers can always be counted.

Q: What's always ahead of you but you can never see?

A: The future

Q: Where can you find, cities, towns, countries, and shops but no people?

A: A map

Q: Bob walked for half an hour in the rain and didn't get a hair on his head wet. He didn't have an umbrella or a hat. How did he do it?
A: He is bald.

Q: I cannot hear even though I have ears. What am I?
A: Corn

Q: There are no doors or windows in this kind of room. What room is this?
A: A mushroom

Q: What do you take in when it isn't being used, but throw out when you need to use it?
A: An anchor

Q: I have difficulty standing up by myself even though I have thousands of legs. I don't have a head even if my neck is long. What am I?
A: I'm a broom.

Q: I can't walk although I have legs.
A: A table

Q: What never moves but always goes up?
A: Stairs

Q: Which side does an egg fall when it was laid by a rooster at the top of a barn?

A: A rooster can't lay eggs. Hens do.

Q: When is a door not a door?

A: When it's ajar

Q: You can't hold me. You can only catch me. What am I?

A: A cold

Q: What can be deadly and quick while it gathers by the beach?

A: Sand

Q: Be careful! You are at a railroad crossing. Be sure that there are no cars. Can you spell this without any 'r's'?

A: T-H-I-S

Q: I have no door, but I hold keys. I have no place to stay even though I have some space. You aren't allowed to leave even if you can enter me. What am I?

A: I'm a keyboard.

Q: I can run and drop but can't walk. What am I?

A: A drop of water

Q: If there are five apples and you take two, how many do you have?
A: You have two.

Q: I have wings, and I can fly. I am not a bird, so what am I?
A: An airplane

Q: What is always late and never present?
A: Later

Q: I can be big, white, dirty, or wicked. What am I?
A: A lie

Q: What do cats, dogs, fish, and turtles all have in common?
A: The letter 'S'

Q: Almost everybody needs me, asks for me, gives me but hardly anyone takes me. What am I?
A: Advice

Q: What am I that can point in every direction, but I can't get anywhere by myself?
A: Your finger

Q: I am not your clothes, but I cover your body. What am I that get thinner the more that I am used?

A: A bar of soap

Q: What am I that never break even if I fall?

A: Nightfall

Q: I'm known as the first of all of my kind. I am never found in trucks and never on buses. I'm not used in Ohio, but I am used in Arkansas.

A: The letter 'A'

Q: I have two backbones and thousands upon thousands of ribs.

A: A railroad

Q: I will always point you in the right direction. You must follow my lead or you will get astray. What am I that will never say more than two words at a time?

A: The signage of 'one way'

Q: I can run constantly without getting tired. I frustrate people without having to move. What am I?

A: A runny nose

Q: What am I that the more of me you leave behind, the more of me you take.

A: I'm footsteps.

Q: I'm heavy forward, but backward I am not. What am I?

A: I'm a ton.

Q: What am I that get bigger the more you've taken from me?

A: I'm a hole.

Q: What am I that if I'm with you, you will want to tell me. But once you tell me, I am no longer with you.

A: I'm a secret.

Q: Everyone has a view of me but doesn't pay attention. Without one, though, everyone would look crazy. What am I?

A: I'm a nose.

Q: It will be harder for you to grab me the more you move with me.

A: Your breath

Q: Do what he says, and you will be okay. Don't and you will lose the game. Who is he?

A: Simon

Q: Bugs don't like this vegetable. It may be the only one they don't move toward. What is it?

A: It's a squash.

Q: You can see me in the water sometimes, but I am always dry.

A: A reflection

Q: I only repeat the last word you say. The more I repeat, the softer I get. I can't be seen but I can be heard. What am I?

A: An echo

Q: Take me for a spin, and I will make you cool. If you use me in the winter, you are a fool. What am I?

A: A fan

Q: You can't really see me, but you can touch me. You can't throw me away but you can throw me out.

A: Your back

Q: What am I that will halt on green and continue on red when you are dealing with me?

A: I'm a watermelon.

Q: Shadows follow me wherever I go. I have no eyes but I can produce tears. I have no wings but I can glide above you. What am I?

A: I'm a cloud.

Q: He says I love you when I told him. He smiles back at me when I smile at him and looks back at me when I look at him. Who is he?
A: His reflection

Q: I go around all cities, towns, and villages but I never go inside anywhere.
A: A road

Q: What do you think I am that can die when I have no life?
A: A battery

Q: When you wave my flag, I took and give away the one you receive?
A: I'm a mailbox.

Q: I'm a five-letter word and very big and hard. I am alone when two letters are removed from me.
A: Stone

Q: I know a word that has six letters. Take away just one letter, twelve is what remains. What word am I?
A: Dozens

Q: Wash me and then I'm not clean. Don't wash me and I am.

A: Water

Q: I live without needing to breathe but I'm always cold. I am never dehydrated but I am hardly ever drinking. What am I?

A: I'm a fish.

Q: At the same time, I go down and up. I am present-tense and past-tense, too. What am I?

A: See-saw

Q: I always run, but there is no way I can walk. I sometimes make small noises but I am not talking. I also have a bed, but I never use it. I never eat but I have a mouth. What am I?

A: A river

Q: When I am changing my jacket, loud noises will be made. I begin to weigh less the more I become larger. What am I?

A: Popcorn

Q: What am I that becomes dirty when I'm white.

A: A blackboard

Q: I shave 30 times a day, but I still have hair.

A: A barber

Q: I do not have a head, but I have a long straight neck. What am I?

A: A bottle

Q: I stay where I am when I go off. What am I?

A: An alarm clock

Q: I do not ask questions but I need an answer.

A: A telephone

Q: What am I that go up and down all of the time, but I never move?

A: The temperature

Q: What do you think I am when I am weightless and as large as an elephant? What am I?

A: I'm an elephant's shadow.

Q: It is not wanted by the person who carved it. It's not needed yet by the person who bought it. It was never seen by the person who used it. What is this thing?

A: A coffin

Q: What do you call a thing that has a head and a foot but has 4 legs?

A: A bed

Q: You can never eat me for lunch or dinner. What am I?

A: Breakfast

Q: What do you call me when you can hold me without touching me?

A: A conversation

Q: I don't need to eat but I have teeth. What do you call me?

A: A comb

Q: What do you call something that can be made but cannot be seen?

A: Noise

Q: Orange is my color and I sound like a parrot. What am I?

A: Carrot

Q: I have flies and four wheels. What do you call me?

A: A garbage pick-up truck

Q: Which part of the turkey has the most feathers?

A: The outside

Chapter 2: Kids' Knock-Knock Jokes

Knock, knock

Who's there?

Figs.

Figs who?

Figs the doorbell, it's not working right!

Knock, knock

Who's there?

Beef.

Beef who?

Beefore it gets too cold, let me in!

Knock, knock

Who's there?

Lettuce.

Lettuce who?

Lettuce inside!

Knock, knock

Who's there?

Olive.

Olive who?

Olive next door?

Knock, knock
Who's there?
Ice cream.
Ice cream who?
Ice cream for ice cream!

Knock, knock
Who's there?
Turnip.
Turnip who?
Turnip the volume, I can't hear anything!

Knock, knock
Who's there?
Orange.
Orange who?
Orange you working on your project?

Knock, knock

Who's there?
Mustache
Mustache who?

I mustache you something but I'll shave it for later if you won't open the door for me!

Who's there?
Annie.
Annie who?
You don't believe Annie thing I say!

Knock, knock
Who's there?
Voodoo.
Voodoo who?
Voodoo you want to go with on your prom?

Knock, knock
Who's there?
Candice.
Candice who?
Candice be the right thing to say?

Knock, knock
Who's there?
Donut.
Donut who?
Donut ask anyone around here.

Knock, knock

Who's there?

Ada.

Ada who?

Ada spaghetti on my meal.

Knock, knock

Who's there?

Anita.

Anita who?

Anita buy shoes, please?

Knock, knock

Who's there?

Annie.

Annie who?

Annie body going to let me in?

Knock, knock

Who's there?

Ben.

Ben who?

Ben singing that song three times. Cut it out already!

Knock, knock

Who's there?

Frank.

Frank who?

I want to Frank you for making me smile.

Knock, knock

Who's there?

Doris.

Doris who?

Doris open, come in.

Knock, knock

Who's there?

Howard.

Howard who?

Howard you guess what that is?

Knock, knock

Who's there?

Isabell.

Isabell who?

Isabell ringing? Somebody might be outside.

Knock, knock

Who's there?

Justin.

Justin who?

Justin town. I have to check on some things.

Knock, knock

Who's there?

Ken

Ken who?

Ken I have more soup, please?

Knock, knock

Who's there?

Lena.

Lena who?

Lena bit closer and you'll know who.

Knock, knock

Who's there?

Nana.

Nana who?

Nana my things are missing.

Knock, knock

Who's there?

Nobel,

Nobel who?

Nobel. That's why I have been knocking for quite some time now.

Knock, knock

Who's there?

Windy.

Windy who?

Windy dog ran, it bumped on my knee.

Knock, knock

Who's there?

Will.

Will who?

Will I meet the man of my dreams someday?

Knock, knock

Who's there?

Cow go.

Cow go who?

No, cow go moo! A cow never said who.

Knock, knock

Who's there?

Goat.

Goat who?

Goat to the pharmacy and buy me some medicine, please.

Knock, knock

Who's there?

Some bunny.

Some bunny who?

Some bunny has finally won the jackpot prize!

Knock, knock

Who's there?

Amarillo.

Amarillo who?

Amarillo kind friend.

Knock, knock

Who's there?

Amish.

Amish who?

Amish our old days.

Knock, knock

Who's there?

Avenue.

Avenue who?

Avenue done makeup before?

Knock, knock
Who's there?
Cash.
Cash who?
I prefer eating peanuts than cash who.

Knock, knock
Who's there?
Dishes.
Dishes who?
Dishes a great place you've got.

Knock, knock
Who's there?
Doctor.
Doctor who?
That is such a great show!

Knock, knock
Who's there?
I'm too short to reach the doorbell.
I'm too short to reach the doorbell who?
No, really. I'm too short.

Knock, knock

Who's there?

Dozen.

Dozen who?

Dozen one know who holds the keys?

Knock, knock

Who's there?

Leaf.

Leaf who?

Leaf him alone. He's wounded.

Knock, knock

Who's there?

Howl.

Howl who?

Howl you remember me when I'm gone?

Knock, knock

Who's there?

Needle.

Needle who?

Do you needle bit help on your homework?

Knock, knock

Who's there?

Police.

Police who?

Police, may I have some cash?

Knock, knock

Who's there?

Radio.

Radio who?

I'm coming up, either you're radio or not.

Knock, knock

Who's there?

Water.

Water who?

Water you doing out there?

Knock, knock

Who's there?

Tank.

Tank who?

Tank you for welcoming me here.

Knock, knock

Who's there?

Witches.

Witches who?

Witches the simplest method to use?

Knock, knock

Who's there?

Wooden shoe.

Wooden shoe who?

Wooden shoe be happier if she's here?

Knock, knock

Who's there?

Harry.

Harry who?

Harry now or else I'll leave you behind.

Knock, knock

Who's there?

Canoe.

Canoe who?

Canoe please help me carry these things?

Knock, knock

Who's there?

I am.

I am who?

How do you not know who you are!

Knock, knock

Who's there?

Yah.

Yah who?

Google is what I prefer.

Knock, knock

Who's there?

Alpaca.

Alpaca who?

Alpaca a first aid kit for our trip tomorrow just to be sure.

Knock, knock

Who's there?

See, you forgot me already!

Knock, knock

Who's there?

Owl says.

Owl says who?

Yes, they do.

Knock, knock

Who's there?

Kanga

Kanga who?

It's not kanga who, it's a kangaroo.

Knock, knock

Who's there?

Beats

Beats who?

Beats me.

Knock, knock

Who's there?

Deja.

Deja who?

Knock, knock

Knock, knock

Who's there?

A broken pencil.

A broken pencil who?

It's pointless, so don't worry about it.

Knock, knock

Who's there?

Europe.

Europe who?

No, I'm not a poo! You're the poo!

Knock, knock

Who's there?

Theodore.

Theodore who?

Theodore was open that's why the thief entered easily.

Knock, knock

Who's there?

Etchy.

Etchy who?

Bless you!

Knock, knock

Who's there?

Spell.

Spell who?

W-H-O.

Knock, knock

Knock, knock

Who's there?

Mikey.

Mikey who?

I left Mikey on the car.

Knock, knock

Who's there?

Herd.

Herd who?

I herd you call my name. Why?

Knock, knock

Who's there?

Venice.

Venice who?

Venice she going to school?

Knock, knock

Who's there?

Iran.

Iran who?

Iran straight from the grocery store.

Knock, knock

Who's there?

Adore.

Adore who?

Adore is open last night.

Knock, knock

Who's there?

Orange.

Orange who?

Orange you going to say you love me before you leave?

Chapter 3: Kids' Silly, Dumb Jokes

Q: A sleeping dinosaur is called what?

A: A dino-snore!

Q: What is fast but loud and crunchy at the same time?

A: A rocket-chip!

Q: Why did the teddy bear pass on dessert?

A: He was stuffed!

Q: What has thousands of ears, but it cannot hear?

A: A cornfield!

Q: What did the left eye say to the right eye?

A: There's something between us and it smells!

Q: What do you get when you come across a vampire and a snowman?

A: Frost-bite!

Q: What was said to the fork by the plate?

A: Dinner is on me!

Q: What is the reason behind the small boy eating his homework?
A: He heard from his teacher that it was a piece of cake!

Q: When you are looking for something, why is it always in the last place you look?
A: Because when you find it, you stop looking for it!

Q: Two pickles fell out of a jar and onto the counter. What did one say to the other?
A: Dill with it.

Q: After eating their supper, how did the Dalmatians react?
A: That hit the spot!

Q: Why did the group of kids cross the park?
A: They needed to get to the other slide!

Q: How does a vampire start writing a letter?
A: Tomb it may concern!

Q: What do you call a droid that takes a different route?
A: R2 detour

Q: How do you stop the astronaut baby from crying?
A: You rocket back and forth!

Q: What was the witches' favorite subject in middle school?

A: Spelling!

Q: How do you make a lemon drop?

A: You let the lemon fall!

Q: What do you call a duck that gets 100% on all of its school projects?

A: A wise quacker!

Q: What kind of water cannot freeze?

A: Hot water!

Q: What sort of tree fits in your hand?

A: A palm tree!

Q: Why did the cracker go to the hospital?

A: Because he felt really crummy!

Q: Why did the baby strawberry start crying?

A: Because its mom and dad were in a jam!

Q: What was the question being asked to the mommy corn by the baby corn?

A: Where is popcorn?

Q: What is worse than raining cats and dogs?

A: Hailing taxis!

Q: Where would you find a penguin?

A: Wherever you lost him!

Q: Which animal is always at a baseball game?

A: A bat!

Q: What always falls in winter but never gets hurt?

A: Snow!

Q: What do you call a ghost's true love?

A: His ghoulfriend!

Q: What building in Los Angeles has the most stories?

A: The public library!

Q: How do you know the ocean is friendly or not?

A: See if it waves!

Q: What is a tornado's favorite game to play at parties?

A: Twister!

Q: How does the moon cut his hair?

A: Eclipse it!

Q: How do you get a squirrel to like you?
A: You gotta act like a nutcase!

Q: What do you call two birds in love?
A: Tweethearts!

Q: How does a scientist freshen his breath?
A: He experi-mints!

Q: How are false teeth like stars?
A: They come out at night!

Q: How can you tell a vampire is getting sick?
A: He starts coffin!

Q: Finding that in your apple, there's a complete worm is less bad than what?
A: Finding a worm cut in half! That means you already ate half!

Q: What is a computer's favorite snack?
A: Computer chips!

Q: What did the cow hear from the apple?

A: Nothing. Apples cannot speak!

Q: When does a cucumber become a pickle?
A: Whenever it goes through a jarring experience!

Q: What do you think of that new diner on the mood?
A: The food was okay, but the atmosphere was awful!

Q: What is the reason why a balloon cannot be given to Elsa?
A: The reason is that it will be let go by her!

Q: How do you make the octopus laugh?
A: With ten-tickles!

Q: What did the finger hear from the nose?
A: Don't pick on me anymore!

Q: Why did the little girl bring a ladder to school?
A: Because she wanted to go to high school!

Q: What is a vampire's favorite fruit?
A: A blood orange!

Q: What do elves learn in English class?
A: The elf-abet!

Q: Why can't the karaoke be sung by the pony?

A: Because his voice was a little hoarse!

Q: Why are school dances being avoided by the skeleton?

A: Because he had no body to dance with!

Q: What do you call a pair of bananas?

A: Slippers

Q: Why is the doctor visited by the banana?

A: Because the banana doesn't peel well.

Q: A fake noodle is called what?

A: An impasta!

Q: How do you fix a cracked pumpkin?

A: You use a pumpkin patch!

Q: What sort of award did the dentist receive?

A: A little plaque!

Q: A sticky hair is a characteristic of bees because?

A: A honeycomb is what they use!

Q: An example of bad liars is the ghost. What is the reason for this?

    A: Because they are transparent!

Q: How was the small flower greeted by the big flower?

A: Hey, bud!

Q: What did the astronaut say when he crashed into the planet?

A: I Apollo-gize!

Q: Why did the orange lose the race?

A: He ran out of juice!

Q: Which dinosaur has the best vocabulary?

A: The thesaurus!

Q: What did one strand of DNA say to her boyfriend strand of DNA?

A: Do these genes make my butt look big?

Q: Why didn't the dogs want to dance at the ball?

A: They have two left feet!

Q: What was being said to the toilet friend from a healthy toilet?

A: You seem a bit flushed!

Q: What is the reason the woman put her money in the freezer?

A: She wanted some cold hard cash!

Q: Why couldn't the astronaut book a room on the moon?

A: Because the moon was full!

Q: What do you call a snowman that is getting old?

A: Water!

Q: Why did the superhero flush his toilet?

A: Because it was his doody!

Q: Where do cows go for entertainment?

A: The mooo-vies!

Q: What does a spider's bride wear?

A: A webbing dress!

Q: What is the smartest creature on earth?

A: A spelling bee

Q: How did the preschoolers learn how to make banana splits?

A: They went to sundae school!

Q: What is the absolute worst thing about throwing a party in space?

A: You have to plan it!

Q: Why did the policeman go to the baseball game?
A: Because he overheard someone had stolen a base so he went to check it out!

Q: Two pairs of pant are worn by golfers at the tournament. What is the reason for this?
A: It was in case they got a hole in one!

Q: What sort of shoes do robbers wear?
A: Sneak-ers!

Q: What do you call two guys hanging out on a curtain?
A: Curt and Rod

Q: Why was the Math book so sad?
A: It was dealing with too many problems!

Q: What time would it be when Godzilla came to hang out?
A: Time to run!

Q: Why did the dog do so well in school?
A: Because he was the teacher's pet!

Q: Why did the egg get thrown out of class?

A: Because he wouldn't stop telling yolks!

Q: What did one penny say to the other while having a conversation?

A: We make perfect cents!

Q: What is the reason behind arresting the belt?

A: Because some pants were being held up by it!

Q: Why did the computer go to the hospital?

A: It became sick with a virus!

Q: Where does the president keep his armies?

A: In his sleeves!

Q: What remark did one firefly receive from the other?

A: You're glowing, girl!

Q: Why did the cucumber blush?

A: He saw the salad dressing!

Q: What do you call a blind dinosaur?

A: Do-you-think-he-saw-us!

Q: How do you catch an entire school of fish?

A: With bookworms!

Q: Why did the mushroom like to party so much?
A: Because he was fungi!

Q: What do you call a guy lying on the front porch?
A: Matt

Q: What do snowmen call their annual ball?
A: The snowball!

Q: If you've seen a spaceman, what will you do?
A: I will be parking my car.

Q: What do cows read?
A: Cattle-logs

Q: Where do young cows eat lunch?
A: In the calf-ateria!

Q: What did the policeman say to his stomach?
A: Stop! You are under a vest!

Q: What do birds give out in their Christmas stockings?
A: Tweets!

Q: How do mountains stay warm in the winter?

A: Snowcaps!

Q: How did the calendar become well-liked?

A: Because he went on so many dates!

Q: What is the reason why the broom is not always on time?

A: It over swept!

Q: Near the sea is where seagulls prefer to live. What is the reason behind this?

A: They will be bagels if they will live by the bay?

Q: After tripping and falling over, what did the horse exclaimed?

A: I fell and can't giddy up!

Q: The girl volcano heard this from the boy volcano. What is it?

A: I lava you!

Q: Name the kind of car that is driven by the girlfriend of Mickey Mouse.

A: A Minnie-van

Q: When you see a sick bird, what will you give it?

A: A special tweetment!

Q: Fishes are wise. Why is that?
A: Because they are always in schools!

Q: What animal has more lives than a cat?
A: A frog. They croak every night!

Q: What musical instrument is always in the bathroom next to the sink?
A: A tuba toothpaste!

Q: Where do pencils take vacations?
A: Pencil-vania!

Q: What kind of music do rabbits and frogs like the best?
A: Hip-hop!

Q: Eight heard this from zero. What is it?
A: Nice belt!

Q: The neck scarf heard this from the snowcap. What is it?
A: Hey, neck scarf, hang around. I will go up ahead.

Q: What time of day do ducks wake up?

A: They wake up at the quack of dawn!

Q: What does the lion say when he first meets another animal in the jungle?
A: Hi, I'm a lion. Pleased to eat you!

Q: What types of markets do dogs and cats hate?
A: Flea-markets!

Q: What do you call a bear that is slowly losing its teeth?
A: You call it a gummy bear.

Q: What do you call a pig that practices martial arts?
A: A porkchop

Q: When a cow is caught in a tornado, what do you call it?
A: A milkshake

Q: When you see a sleeping bull, what do you call it?
A: A bulldozer

Q: Tell me the difference between climate and weather.
A: You are able to climb it but you cannot weather a tree.

Q: What does the tree wear to the summer pool parties?

A: Swimming trunks!

Q: Why did the sun go to school?
A: To get brighter!

Q: How does a ghost stay safe when he is driving?
A: He puts on his sheet belt!

Q: What do monsters turn on in the summer time?
A: Their scare conditioner!

Q: What is scarecrows' favorite food?
A: Strawberries!

Q: What kind of monster loves the disco?
A: The boogieman!

Q: Why do witches always say their name when they start a conversation?
A: So they know which witch is which!

Q: How do you make a witch itch?
A: Take away the 'W'

Q: Why is it always safe to tell a mummy your secrets?

A: Because they will keep it under wraps!

Q: Which of Santa's reindeer has an attitude problem?
A: Rude-olph!

Q: What is Frosty the Snowman's favorite type of cereal?
A: Frosted Flakes

Q: What did the hamburger name her daughter when she was born?
A: Patty!

Q: Where does Superman like to shop for food?
A: At the supermarket!

Q: A cow that has no legs is called?
A: Ground beef!

Q: What did the skeleton order for dinner?
A: Spare ribs!

Q: What is a balloon's least favorite kind of music?
A: Pop music!

Q: Why did the musician get arrested?
A: He got into some treble!

Q: What is a skeleton's favorite instrument?

A: A trombone!

Q: Which punk rock group has four men who can't sing to save their lives?

A: Mount Rushmore!

Q: What sorts of tunes do the planets listen to?

A: Nep-tunes!

Q: A bear that weighs 6,000 pounds should go where?

A: It should go dieting!

Q: Where did two walls meet?

A: On the corner!

Q: Why does a dragon always sleep from 8:00 am to 4:00 pm?

A: So they can fight knights!

Q: Cards cannot be played by pirates. Why is that?

A: Because all over the deck he walks!

Q: Two elevators are talking to each other. What did they say to each other?

A: I am not feeling good. I feel like something is coming down with me.

Q: How is a headache cured?
A: The pane will disappear if you put your head through a window!

Q: Before robbing the bank, the robber took a bath. Why is that?
A: He wants to have a clean get-a-way!

Q: What did two pencils tell one another?
A: You are looking kinda dull. Are you okay?!

Q: Why are frogs always in such a good mood?
A: They just eat whatever bugs them!

Q: What sound do porcupines make when they smooch?
A: Ouch!

Q: What did the blanket say to comfort the bed when he was upset?
A: Don't worry! I got you covered!

Q: This contains thousands of letters, ends in letter E, and begins with letter P. What do you call it?
A: A post office!

Chapter 4: Longer Dumb Jokes

George was on his way home from a party. He was walking down the street when he heard something behind him. It was making a booming noise. BOOM! BOOM! BOOM! He turned around to see a coffin following him! He started running to his house. The coffin kept following him. It got louder and louder! BOOM! BOOM! BOOM! George was frightened. Once he reached the front door of his house, he noticed the coffin right behind him. He quickly unlocked the door and tried to push the coffin out, but it followed him in any way. He ran upstairs to his bedroom and grabbed the first thing he could to throw at the coffin. A bag of cough drops. He threw them, and the coffin stopped.

"Oh no!" the kangaroo said to the snake. "We are supposed to get some rain today!"

"What is wrong with that?" said the snake. "We could use some rain. It's so dry here!"

"It just means my kids are going to have to play inside all day!" groaned the kangaroo.

A woman asked her lawyer about his fees. He told her he charges $100 for every three questions. The woman said that seems like a bit much, don't you think? He replied yes but those are my charges. He asked her what her final question was.

A little girl is sitting at home and hears a knock at the front door. She opens it and screams in disgust. It was a turtle. She throws it as far as she can and shuts the door. A year later, she hears a knock at the door. She opens it and sees a turtle. He asks, "What was that all about?"

A snail went to a car dealership. The salesman was very surprised that the snail wanted to buy a fast, sportscar. When the snail requested to have the sides of the car painted with a big 'S', the salesman was surprised even more. He asked the snail why he would want something like that. The snail replied, "I want people to say, 'look at that S car go!'"

Three men are driving through the desert when their car breaks down. They each bring an item to take on their hike into town. One of the men grabs a jug of water. The second one takes a box of crackers. The third takes the car door. One of the men says that they can drink the water in case they get thirsty. The other says they can eat the crackers in case they get hungry. The third one says he can roll down the window in case they get hot.

A father and daughter walk into a library. They both look at each other and ask the front desk clerk for two cheeseburgers and two orders of fries. The librarian looks at them and tells them they are in a library. The man says 'Oh' and whispers to the librarian, "We will take two cheeseburgers and two orders of fries."

A small chicken walks into a library and says, "Book, book, book!" The librarian hands the chicken a couple of small paperback books and watches as the chicken leaves the library. He walks across the street, over a hill, and disappears from the librarian's sight.
The next day the same chicken comes into the library and says, "Book, book, book!" The librarian does the same thing. She hands the chicken a few small, paperback books and watches the chicken cross the road and go over the hill. The chicken disappears from her sight again.
The day after that, the chicken walks back into the library and says, "Book, book, book!" She hands the chicken the books but instead of watching the chicken disappear, she follows it. They both cross the street and go over the hill. When they get to the other side of the hill, the librarian watches as the chicken walks up to the biggest frog she has ever seen. The chicken hands the books to the frog and he says, "Read it...read it...read it."

A son and father were sitting down for dinner. The boy turns to his dad and asks, "Dad, are bugs good to eat?"

The dad turns to his son and tells him, "Don't talk about stuff like that at dinner. That is inappropriate while we are eating!"

After the two are done eating dinner, the dad asks his son why he would ask such a question. The boy looks at his father and says, "Well, there was a big bug in your soup, but it's gone now."

Teacher: "If I gave you three cats, plus another two cats, and then another one cat. How many would you have?"

Boy: "Seven."

Teacher: "No, listen carefully. If I gave you three cats, plus two more cats, plus another cat, how many would you have?"

Boy: "Seven."

Teacher: "Okay, let me put this in a different way. If I gave you three oranges, plus two more oranges, and another one orange, how many would you have?

Boy: "Six."

Teacher: "Okay. So, if you have three cats, and I gave you two more, plus one more, how many would you have?"

Boy: "Seven."

Teacher: "No, where are you getting the number seven from?"

Boy: "I already have a cat at home!"

Mr. and Mrs. Shoe had two sons. One was named Mind Your Own Business and the other was named Trouble. The two sons decided to play a game of hide-and-seek. Trouble went to go hide while Mind

Your Own Business counted down from one hundred. Mind Your Own Business started searching for his brother everywhere. He looked underneath cars. He looked in bushes and around in a dark alley near their house. A police officer walked up to him and asked him what he was doing. "I'm playing a game," replied the brother. The policeman asked him what his name was to which the boy replied, "Mind Your Own Business." The police officer grew angry. He said, "Listen, son. Are you looking for Trouble?" Mind Your Own Business replied, "Yes. Actually, I am."

A teacher asks her students to make a sentence using the word 'beans'. One small girl spoke up and said, "My mom cooks beans at home." Another little girl stood up and said, "My father grows his own beans in our garden." A third little girl stood up and said, "We are all human beans."

A robber goes into a bank and holds everyone hostage. He says, "Give me all of your money or your chemistry!" One of the bank tellers says, "Don't you mean history?" The robber tells the bank teller, "Don't change the subject!"

Him: "Oh, no! I just fell off a 50ft ladder!"
Her: "Oh, wow! Are you okay?"
Him: "Yeah, I fell off of the first step."

One night, a queen and a king went into the castle. There was no one in the castle and no one ever came out of it. The next morning, three people walked out of the castle. Who were they? The knight, the queen, and the king.

A man was driving down the road when a policeman stopped him. When the officer approached the car, he asked the man why he had penguins in the backseat? The man replied, "These are my penguins. They belong to me." The officer said that the man needs to take them to the zoo. The next day, the police officer saw the same man driving down the road. He pulled him over to make sure he had taken the penguins to the zoo. This time, when he saw the man and the penguins, they all had sunglasses on. The police officer told him, "I thought I told you to take these penguins to the zoo?" He then replied, "I did! Today we are going to the beach!"

One person decided to pay his buddy a visit. When he arrived at his house, his mouth dropped. A dog and his friend were focused on a game of chess. The man said, "That is amazing! This has to be the smartest dog in the entire world." His friend replied. "No, not really. I've won the last three out of five games!"

A spell was put over a prince. He is only allowed to speak just a word every year. He can speak two words in a year if he doesn't speak a word the previous year, and so forth. He then met a pretty woman one day. In order for him to tell her, "my dear," he decided to not speak to her for two years. He also wants her to know that he loves her. So, before he could say anything to her, he needs to wait again for three years. After five years, he wants to ask her to marry him. So, he still needs to wait for four more years. At last, after nine years, the man can finally say, "My dear, I love you. Will you marry me?" The beautiful woman said, "I'm sorry. I didn't hear you. What?"

Connor went to go visit his 90-year old grandpa who lived far out in the country. He was going to stay for a couple of days. The first morning, his grandpa made Connor a plate full of bacon and eggs. Connor felt a weird film on the plate. He asked his grandpa if the plate was clean. His grandpa replied, "They are as clean as Cold Water can get them!" The next morning, Connor's grandpa made toast and sausage. Connor saw some left-over egg on the plate. He asked his grandpa if the plates were clean and his grandpa assured him they were. He said, "They are as clean as Cold Water can get them."

Connor was getting ready to leave his grandpa's house. When he was on his way to the front door, his grandpa's dog stopped him and began growling. Connor yelled at his grandpa, "Grandpa! Your dog won't let me leave!" His grandpa yells back, "Cold Water, go lie down! Let Connor leave."

Four men are waiting in a hospital lobby while their wives are having babies. The first nurse comes out of the room and yells at the first man. "Congratulations, you have twins!"

The man replies, "That's funny. I work for the Minnesota Twins!"

The second nurse comes out of the room and yells at the second man.

"Congratulations, you have triplets!"

The second man replies, "That's funny. I work for the 3M Company!"

The third nurse comes out of the room and yells at the third man. "Congratulations, you have quadruplets!"

The third man replies, "That's funny. I work for The Four Seasons hotel."

The last man begins crying. All of the other men look at him and ask him what is wrong.

"The last man replies, "I work for 7-Up."

The teacher asked little Bobby if he knew his numbers. He replied yes.

"Good!" the teacher says. "What comes after four?"

"Five," says Bobby.

"What about after seven?" replies the teacher.

"Eight," says Bobby.

"How about after nine?" says the teacher.

"Ten," says Bobby with a loud sigh. Bobby was growing bored of the teacher's questions.

"Okay then. What about after ten?" says the teacher.

"Jack," says Bobby.

A man comes home after a long day of work. He opens the fridge to get out a nice, cold soda. Inside, he sees a rabbit taking a little nap. The man carefully wakes up the rabbit.

He asks, "What are you doing in my fridge?"

The rabbit replies, "Isn't this a Westinghouse?"

"Uh, yes," the man replies. "It is."

"Well then," the rabbit replies, "I'm twying to west."

A businessman walked into work one morning to find that some handymen were repainting the building. He noticed that they were all wearing two windbreakers. The businessman found it a bit strange because it was a hot summer's day.

It bothered the businessman so much that he finally left his office and went to ask the handymen why they were wearing two windbreakers.

One of the handymen replied, "The can says, for best results, please use two coats."

A huge cruise ship passes by a small island. All of the passengers see a bearded man on the island running around and flailing his arms.

"Captain," one of the passengers asks, "who is that man over there on the island?"

"I have no idea," the captain replies, "but every time we drive by here, he goes crazy!"

One day, a man walks into the movie theatre with an elephant.

"I'm sorry, sir. I can't allow you to bring in an elephant to the movie theatre," says one of the managers.

"Oh, he is well-behaved! I promise," says the man.

"All right then. If you are one-hundred percent sure," says the manager.

After the movie, the manager walks up to the man. "I'm so surprised. Your elephant was so well-behaved!"

The man says, "I am, too. He hated the book!"

A small boy walked into a restaurant. He saw a sign outside that said fat-free French fries. He thought to himself that they sounded great and he was starving!

"I'll take an order of fat-free French fries," says the boy to the older gentlemen behind the counter.

"Okay, coming right up!" says the older man.

A basket of French fries was being watched by the boy as it was taken out from the fryer by the cook. When the cook placed the potatoes in a box for to-go, oil was still dripping from them.

"Hang on for a second," said the boy. "Those fries don't look fat-free."

"Sure they are," said the man. "We only charge for the potatoes. The fat is completely free."

Two dogs, a Chihuahua and a Dalmatian, were being walked by two friends. Suddenly, when they were near a restaurant, they smelled something amazing coming from it.

The man who owns the Dalmatian asks the other guy if he wants to get something to eat.

"Sure," he says, "but we have dogs with us. They won't let us in."

The guy with the Dalmatian says, "Follow my lead." After putting on a pair of sunglasses, he walked into the restaurant.

'I'm sorry, sir. You can't bring your dog in here," says the manager. "We have a strict no pets policy."

"This is my seeing-eye dog," says the man with the Dalmatian.

"A Dalmatian?" says the manager, confused.

"Yes, they are using Dalmatians now," says the man.

"Very well, then. Come on in," says the manager.

The guy with the Chihuahua follows his friends lead. He puts on some sunglasses and then walked over inside the restaurant.

The manager says, "Sorry, sir. No pets allowed."

The guy says, "but this is my seeing-eye dog."

"A Chihuahua?" says the manager.

"A Chihuahua?!" says the man. "They gave me a Chihuahua?"

Chapter 5: Kids' Puns and Other Jokes

Have you heard about the man that has his entire left side cut off? He is all right now.

My leaf blower just doesn't blow. Man, it sucks.

I'm great friends with twenty-five letters of the alphabet. I don't know why.

Somehow, I have forgotten which side the sun has risen when I woke up this morning. Suddenly, it dawned on me.

A golf ball is always going to be a golf ball. It doesn't matter how you putt it.

Can your dog do magic tricks? Mine can. He's a labracadabrador.

I tried to capture some fog. I mist.

The longer you sleep in a bed, the taller you are.

There was a boomerang joke I heard earlier, and it was really funny. I can't remember it, though. Give me a minute. It'll come back to me.

Some whiteboards are simply remarkable.

What would be the point in the end if you can make both ends of a pencil as erasers?

I was figuring out how lightning is formed as I watched a thunderstorm. Suddenly, it struck me!

A little word of advice. You should never lie to an x-ray technician. They'll always be able to see right through you.

Speed bumps are what I am extremely scared of. You shouldn't worry though. I'll get over it slowly.

I read a sales advertisement that says, "TV for sale, $1, volume stuck on full." I cannot turn that down, I thought.

Wow! That wedding was so emotional. The cake was in tiers.

Broken puppets for sale. No strings attached!

I couldn't have time to search for my lost watch.

Dead batteries were being sold on a shop I happened to pass by. There was absolutely no charge!

A long time ago, I was a soap-addict. Fortunately, I am now cleaned.

The other day, I was walking behind a clown. We both walked into the same shopping store and he opened the door for me. I thought to myself. Man, what a good jester.

The person who invented the knock-knock joke was a genius! Give that guy a no-bell prize!

I used to sing in the shower. It was great fun until I got soap in my mouth. I asked my mom how to stop it from happening. She said stop singing those soap operas.

I would like to make you laugh with my joke about construction, but I forgot the punch line. I am still working on it.

The newly bought stair lift was giving my grandma a lot of problems. It literally drives her up a wall.

I have a gift for the guy who invented the zero. Nothing!

A camouflage shirt is what I really wanted to buy. However, the right one cannot be found.

There are new reversible jackets that recently came out. Have you heard about them? How good they will turn out is a mystery.

I was figuring out how my seatbelt should be properly fastened, but it didn't work. Then it clicked!

A man just assaulted that lady with cow's milk, cheese, and some butter! How dairy!

I didn't know how I felt after my mood ring was stolen by someone.

Some food coloring was what I accidentally swallowed yesterday. When I went to the doctor, he said I was fine. I felt like I dyed a little inside.

I wondered why the baseball got bigger and bigger. And then it hit me!

Some guy was hit by a soda bottle in the head. Luckily, it was a soft drink.

These stairs cannot be trusted. They are always up to no good!

Again, my printer's making some music. I think the paper's jamming.

I saw a snake next to a Lego set the other day. I think he was a boa constructor.

My time machine and I go waaayyyy back!

The drill is known by the dentist's regular visitors.

Since she's always counting, I no longer hang out with my ex-best friend. I wonder what she is up to now!

My sister could not believe that I could make a new car made of noodles, so she made a bet of $100. The look on her face when I rode pasta was satisfying.

I have to put my foot down, finally, when I was told to stop acting a flamingo by my mom.

I have to blame my shelf when a book fell on my head.

A new type of broom came out today. People were standing in line waiting to buy it. It's really sweeping the nation!

My girlfriend quit her job at the donut factory. She was so sick and tired of the hole business.

A boiled egg in the morning is sure hard to beat.

Did you hear about the old Italian waiter? He pasta way last week.

Learning how to collect trash was difficult. I just picked it up as I went on.

My dog loves pizza. His favorite is puperoni.

Children who fail their coloring tests always need a shoulder to crayon.

The spider had to use the computer. He needed to check on his web site.

The Energizer Bunny was arrested. He was charged with battery.

"Doctor, there is a patient on line one who says he is invisible."
"Well, tell him I cannot see him right now."

I was addicted to the Hokey Pokey. Luckily, I turned myself around.

I was grateful that you explained to me the word 'many.' It means a lot.

I accidentally handed my best friend a glue stick instead of Chapstick. Now, he's not talking to me.

How did I get fired from the calendar factory, you may ask? Well, I just wanted to take a day off!

Just don't spell part backward. Trust me, it's a trap!

Did you watch the news? There was a kidnapping at the middle school. Everything is okay, though. He woke up.

A friend of mine tried to annoy me with bird buns, but I realized toucan play that game.

The bike was two-tired to stand up on its own.

If a baby refuses to sleep during nap-time, are they resisting a rest?

Chapter 6: Quirky Questions

Why does the feet smell and nose run?

If it is only happening in North America, then why do they call it The World Series?

Why is it called a building if it is already built?

If practice makes perfect, and nobody is perfect, why should they have to practice?

If a tomato is a fruit, is ketchup a smoothie?

Why is the glue not sticking inside the bottle of the glue?

If number two pencils are the most popular type of pencil, why are they called number twos?

Would seven days without exercise make one weak?

Why do you call it 'rush hour' when the traffic is slow?

Why does our hair lighten and our skin darkens when exposed to the sun?

Why does the watch's third hand call the second hand?

How much deeper would the ocean be without sponges?

How do 'stay off the grass' signs get there in the first place?

Why is it called the Secret Service if everyone knows about it?

If a mime is arrested, do the police have to tell him that he has the right to remain silent?

Why is it called a television set if you only get one TV?

Why do pizza shops put round pizzas into square boxes?

Why apartments are always built together?

Why do we drive on parkways and park in driveways?

Why is mail that gets delivered by the sea called 'CARgo' but mail delivered on land is called 'SHIPments?'

Chapter 7: Books Never Written

"How to fish" by Will Ketchum

"Healthy Foods" by Chris P. Bacon

"Living through the Storms" by Ty Foon

"Musical Instruments" by ZylaFone

"Starting a Fire" by M. Burr

"How to Win a 5k Marathon" by Sprintz A. Lott

"Architecture" by Bill Dhing

"Flying Beasts" by Tara Dactle

"Answering the Door" by Isabelle Rings

"Batman's Worst Enemy" by Joe Kurr

"Learning to Read" by Abe E. Seas

"A Guide to Flying" by Al T. Tude

"Dessert" by Sue Flay

"A Guide to New York" by Dee Big Apple

"A Detective's Case" by Mr. E.

"A Butterfly's Life" by Kat E. Pillar

"Giant Snakes" by Ann A. Conda

"How to Wrestle Bears" by Dan Jerus

"How to Work Out" by Jim Nasium

"Mathematics" by Jean Yuss

"How to be Helpful" by Linda Hand

"A Day at the Beach" by Sandy Feat

"Woodwind Instruments" by Clair E. Nett

"Everything is Going Wrong" by Mel Function

"To the Outhouse" by Willy Mayket; illustrated by Bettee Wont

"Walking to School" by Misty Bus

"Where have all of the Animals Gone?" by Darin DeBarn

"Falling off of a Cliff" by Aileen Dover N. Fell

"I was Prepared" by Justine Kase

"Green Spots on the Walls" by Picken and Flicken

"The Lost Scout" by Werram Eye

'The Bearded Man" by Harry Chin

"Crossing a Man with a Duck" by Willie Waddle

"Raise Your Arms" by Harry Pitts

"Sitting on the Beach" by Sandi C. Heeks

"My Life as a Gas Station Attendant" by Phil R. Awp

"Something Smells" by I Ben Phartin

"Household Book of Tools" by M.C. Hammer

"Late for Work" by Dr. Wages

"Computer Memory" by Meg. A. Byte

"The Future of Robotics" by Ann Droid and Cy B. Org

"What to do if you are in a Car Accident" by Rhea Ender

"Taking Tests" by B. A. Wiseman

"Over the Mountaintop" by Hugo First

Conclusion

Thank you for making through to the end of *Karen's OMG Joke Book for Kids: Funny, Silly, Dumb Jokes that Will Make Children Roll on the Floor Laughing*. Let's hope it was filled with the necessary information to make your child laugh!

This book has been written for younger kids. It isn't just the normal knock-knock jokes, although they are in the book. This book is filled with all sorts of jokes that will surely get your child laughing! There are some that will make them think. Some of them are just really bad puns that will make, even you, shake your head. There are also some classic riddles that are so popular that they've withstood the test of time. You can enjoy it as a family or leave your child to use their imagination. The book is free of dirty jokes and all jokes that use profanity. I hope you enjoyed it!

Finally, if you found this to be a good book, a review on Amazon is always appreciated!

Connect with us on our Facebook page www.facebook.com/bluesourceandfriends and stay tuned to our latest book promotions and free giveaways.

Lightning Source UK Ltd.
Milton Keynes UK
UKHW040024031221
R2920100001B/R29201PG394973UKX00001B/1